Prolific Author

The Step-by-Step Guide to Write More Words in Less Time and Finish Your Book Fast

Author Success Foundations Book 4

by

Christopher di Armani

Copyright © 2018 Christopher di Armani

All rights reserved.

ISBN-13: 978-1988938202

Editor: Nicolas Johnson

Published By:
Botanie Valley Productions Inc.
PO Box 507
Lytton, BC V0K 1Z0
http://BotanieValleyProductions.com

Dedication

This book is dedicated to my sweet and loving wife Lynda. Without her unwavering support none of this would be possible.

Acknowledgments

Without the assistance of my editor, Nicolas Johnson, I can't imagine how this book would read. He tears my words apart from every conceivable angle, then offers thoughtful and constructive criticism on how best to fix the destruction at our feet. I thank God for Nicolas Johnson and his talents, daily.

#EditorsMatter

Feedback Loop

I also wish to express my heartfelt gratitude to the following individuals who took time from their own busy lives to critique this manuscript. Their willingness to assist a total stranger humbles me.

Kim Steadman (KimSteadman.com)
Sharilee Swaity (Facebook.com/Sharilee.Swaity)

Table of Contents

Foreword	1
Understanding What Drives You To Write	5
A Healthy Dose of Encouragement	11
Daily Habits to Generate Success	17
The Great Multi-Tasking Lie	31
Apply Self-Honesty	33
Take Action	41
Download the Free Workbook	44
The Road to Writing Success is Finishing Your Book	45
One Last Thing!	46
About Christopher di Armani	47
Books by Christopher di Armani	48
Appendix - Sample Daily Writing Routine	54
Endnotes	55

Foreword

The first three books in this series taught you:

1. how to develop your author success mindset,

2. how to design your morning routine and enhance your clarity and focus, and

3. how to create your personal author vision statement.

Your author vision statement revealed the legacy you desire for your life. You acknowledged your strengths and weaknesses, applauded your successes and learned from your failures. You gained clarity about what motivates you and what holds you back and keeps you from your dreams. You also clarified your core values - the character traits responsible for every decision you make.

With this foundation in place, it's time to dig deeper and uncover why you do what you do; what drives your compulsion to etch words on the page.

Be clear on why you want to write a book.

If significance, fame and fortune are your desires, there are far easier ways to achieve them than writing a book.

The key to unlock your drive to succeed is knowing why you write. When you understand how your desire to write fulfills your core needs, you transform writing from a chore to be dreaded into the vision you were born to fulfill. Time set aside to write becomes as critical to your life as the food you eat and the water you drink.

We structure meal times for a reason. It ensures we maintain the energy required to fulfill our duties, whatever they may be. So why don't we implement a structure to achieve success? If we believe success does not matter, neither does the road we travel to get there.

Success matters. The road you travel to achieve success matters more.

Your daily writing routine is the last piece of the puzzle to build a life focused on accomplishing your goal - a finished and published book.

You become an unstoppable writer when you fulfill your core needs. This is the natural and inevitable result, but you require structure to build habits and guarantee your success. That structure is your daily writing routine, tailored to the needs and commitments of your life.

When you construct your routine centered around your need to write, you make productivity the norm of your life, instead of the exception it is today. When you develop the habit of writing every day, you propel yourself forward. Your completed manuscript becomes inevitable.

Every writer's life is different. Your ideal daily routine looks nothing like mine, and for good reason. You aren't me. Our lives differ, maybe just a little, maybe by orders of magnitude. Who knows? More important, who cares? It is not our differences that matter - it's our similarities. This book uncovers those similarities, but only when you take action - when you complete the exercises with honesty.

As with every book in this series, you must commit to take action if you want results. Toss it on your bookshelf and your journey down Publication Highway will continue at its current sluggish pace. If this pace satisfied you, even remotely, you would not be here.

If you read any of the earlier books in this series, you already know one thing.

I want you to succeed.

In the pages ahead, you will learn how to create a system designed to push you forward to your goal. Follow this system and I guarantee you will finish your book and publish it, too.

That's a big, bold promise.

How on earth can I guarantee you will do anything? You're right. I can't, but I make my guarantee based on one incontrovertible fact: You bought this book.

Your action - to click the Buy button and part with your hard-earned cash - tells me all I need to know about you. You want to write a book and you know you must change something to get it done.

You also understand my expectations.

A person, reluctant to change and unwilling to heed sound advice, does not purchase this book, nor do I want them to. I don't care about royalties from dreamers, the would-be writers of the world. My goal is far greater.

I want a tsunami of prolific writers.

Anyone can write. Not everyone is willing to change their lives to fulfill their destiny.

You are.

Excellent.

I have a lot of ground to cover. Some is familiar, some is not. It is all designed to help you construct a clear roadmap for your journey down Publication Highway.

Chapter 1

Understanding What Drives You To Write

Introduction

According to a variety of sources, 80-97% of people want to write a book. Less than 3% ever complete their manuscript and of this pathetic number, only 20% publish their books.

These numbers paint a bleak picture, yet here we are, determined to beat these terrible odds.

You are not 80-97% of people.

Honest self-examination holds no interest for those who want a fast lane to fame and fortune. One look at the title of this book and they're gone. Good riddance to those posers, too.

Your willingness is a reflection of your commitment. Embrace it. Fan the flames of your passion to write until the raging fire burns away all your fear and trepidation.

Now, let's examine what drives us to do the things we do. Let's determine which of the six core human needs drive your life. Your core needs are like gasoline, they power your journey down Publication Highway to your destination - your published book.

Maslow's Hierarchy of Needs

To understand your unconscious drives and motivations, I'll begin with Abraham Maslow's 1943 paper, *A Theory of Human Motivation*[1], first published in Psychological Review.

Maslow sought to understand why human beings do what we do. No small challenge, yet he succeeded beyond his own wildest dreams. Our current generation of life coaches and motivational speakers built their immensely successful businesses upon his work.

Maslow's original hierarchy of needs five-stage model includes:

1. Biological and physiological needs - air, food, drink, shelter, warmth, sex, sleep.
2. Safety needs - protection from the elements, security, order, law, stability, freedom from fear.
3. Love and belonging needs - trust and acceptance, friendship, intimacy, receiving and giving affection and love. Affiliating, being part of a group, such as family, friends, or work.
4. Esteem needs - which Maslow classified into two categories: esteem for oneself (dignity, achievement, mastery, independence) and the desire for reputation or respect from others.
5. Self-actualization needs - realizing personal potential, seeking personal growth and peak experiences, self-fulfillment - a desire "to become everything one is capable of becoming" (Maslow, 1987, p. 64).

In his later years, Maslow expanded his hierarchy and split it into two major sets, deficiency needs and growth needs. Deficiency needs are the bottom four levels of the pyramid.

1. Physiological
2. Safety
3. Love and Belonging
4. Esteem
5. Growth needs comprise the upper four levels.
6. Cognitive
7. Aesthetic
8. Self-actualization
9. Transcendence.

According to Maslow, individuals must meet the needs at the lower levels of the pyramid before they can successfully be motivated to tackle the next levels. The lowest four levels represent deficiency needs, and the upper three levels represent growth needs.[2]

The most basic human need, survival, motivates us to obtain the essentials of life - food, water, shelter, heat, and so on. Once those needs are met, we can focus on our personal safety and security - the need to ensure we have a safe place to live, food to eat and water to drink.

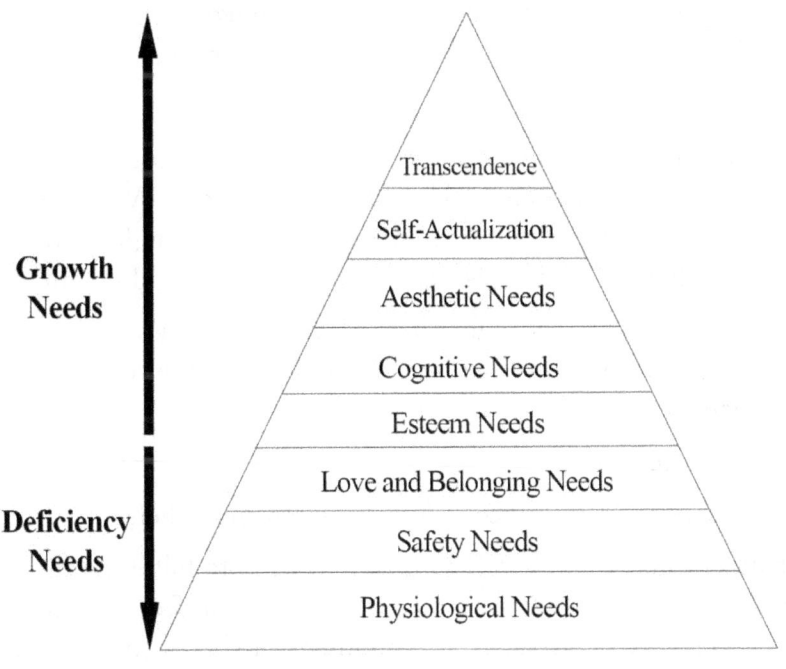

When those fundamental needs are not met, we will risk personal safety and security to meet them. We will do what is required to meet those needs with little or no thought to consequence if the situation is dire. For example, a starving person will steal, harm or kill anyone who gets in the way of their need for food.

Only when our personal safety is assured, do we open up to possibility of finding friends and loved ones, and our need for social interaction with others. If our first two levels of needs are unfulfilled, we'll risk loved ones, friends and societal status and belonging to fulfill them.

These levels are not, as Maslow first proposed, mutually exclusive. Human beings are motivated by a range across all levels of Maslow's hierarchy, often simultaneously. You can still meet your higher needs even when one or more lower need remains unfulfilled.

Tony Robbins on 6 Core Needs

Anthony Robbins, the ultra-successful author and life coach, took Maslow's hierarchy and reworked it into his signature six core needs[3] theory of human motivation.

1. Certainty / Comfort

The need for certainty equates to Maslow's biological and physiological needs for food, drink, shelter, sleep and freedom from fear.

2. Uncertainty / Variety

This is the opposite of the need for certainty and comfort, and manifests in our desire for excitement and boredom with routine. We all need food to survive, but if our food requirement is met by a single food source, we become bored and dissatisfied. We want something different to eat.

The same is true of our need for safety. Once our safety is assured, we seek ways to push our perceived limits and boundaries. We seek excitement and danger.

3. Significance

How we achieve significance is determined by our beliefs.

Disparate beliefs result in wildly diverse actions to fulfill the same core need. One set of beliefs lands a man on the moon or feeds the homeless. Another belief flies airplanes into buildings or shoots strangers from a university campus clock tower. The path to fulfill the core need is different, but the core need, significance, remains the same.

4. Love and Connection

This incorporates our needs for friendship, intimacy, trust and acceptance, receiving and giving affection and love, and being part of a group, such as family, friends, or work.

5. Growth

Our need for growth fuels our desire to improve our life conditions through self-improvement. This also drives our need for peak experiences, such as the athlete's desire to win an Olympic gold medal or a man's need to overcome self-imposed and self-defeating thoughts to achieve success at work.

6. Contribution

Every philanthropist in history fulfilled their need for contribution through their charitable works. Those works also met their need for significance, love and compassion.

No single need operates in isolation.

The first four – certainty, variety, significance, love and connection – cover our basic physical and psychological needs. We all need food, water, a job, excitement, someone to love and who loves us. The last two – our need for personal growth and contribution to society – usually reveal themselves after our more urgent needs are met.

I believe most authors rank high in their need for both significance and contribution. We believe our message is important, hence our desire to share it with the world. We want to give back and help others, hence our need to contribute.

I recommend listening to Tony Robbins' 30-minute audio discussion[4] on why we do what we do. It will give you a solid foundation in his core needs model and help clarify the forces driving your own life, both good and bad.

Our Life is Defined by Our Conditions and Our Blueprint

"Our life is defined by our conditions and our blueprint," says Anthony Robbins.

Our life conditions are the things we do, the place we live, where we work, the people we are in relationship with, etc. These conditions exist because of our personal beliefs, or using Robbins' vernacular, our blueprint.

Our blueprint is our belief system. It is what we value, combined with how tight we cling to those values no matter what happens in our lives.

As I discussed in book one of this series, Awaken Your Author Mindset To Finish Writing Your Book Fast, our mind is the most magnificent computer ever created. Our mind believes everything we tell it, without exception. Unfortunately, because it cannot discern between "positive" and "negative" thoughts and believes every thought without question, our mind executes based on the input received. This, in turn, creates our reality.

When we build our self-confidence with positive messages we achieve incredible feats. When we tell ourselves negative thoughts, our mind believes the most self-destructive lies and destroys our world.

As a result, it's often through pain we decide to change our lives.

Would you read this book if you did not experience pain and failure at your inability to complete your book? No, you purchased this book with the hope I could provide answers to solve your problem and take away your pain.

I struggle with the same issues as you.

Procrastination and lack of self-discipline are my daily challenges. I must fight and win these battles every single day. Systems help.

The path forward is simple.

Make a decision. Follow your decision with action.

I fail at the action phase. I know my shortcomings, so I build structure into my day. I form habits to write every day. This structure and the habits I build upon it mean I'm better equipped, mentally and Simple, but not easy, just like the rest of life.

Chapter 2
A Healthy Dose of Encouragement

Anyone Can Write A Book

Anyone can write a book and achieve fame and fortune, as the long list of authors who started with the deck stacked against them proves.

When you lack inspiration and motivation to write, when you believe you are not good enough or smart enough or educated enough to write, read the following mini-biographies to understand, deep in your heart, why you are full of crap.

Take heed of the work ethic, self-discipline and sheer strength of will each of these writers possessed. They refused to fail, no matter what life threw at them.

Odds are your life is easier than theirs. Odds are you're better educated, too.

Follow their examples.

Do what they did, and you, too, will share their success.

You, like me, already possess every quality needed to accomplish your goals.

Are you as committed to writing as these authors? Do you possess the strength of will, the depth of character, and the determination to take every action required to achieve your goals?

Excellent.

Will you put those qualities to work today?

Ray Bradbury

"The great fun in my life has been getting up every morning and rushing to the typewriter because some new idea has hit me. The feeling I have every day is very much the same as it was when I was twelve. In any event, here I am, eighty years old, feeling no different, full of a great sense of joy, and glad for the long life that has been allowed me. I have good plans for the next ten or twenty years, and I hope you'll come along."

Ray Bradbury is one of the world's most famous and successful authors.

He barely managed to graduate from high school, and although his formal education ended there, his informal education did not. He read voraciously. He spent evenings in the public library where he devoured every text about the subject currently holding his interest. He spent his days in the library basement, where he rented a typewriter by the hour. The pressure of this deadline forced him to focus with great intensity to complete his story before the hour passed.

He desired to be a writer and refused to allow any obstacle to stop him from achieving his goal. Success, fame and fortune are the rewards for his tenacity, perseverance and self-discipline.

Mark Twain

"There is nothing training cannot do. Nothing is above its reach. It can turn bad morals to good; it can destroy bad principles and recreate good ones; it can lift men to 'angel ship.'"

Born Samuel Langhorne Clemens on November 30, 1835, he wrote American literary masterpieces under the pen name Mark Twain, steamboat slang for 12 feet of water.

His formal education ended at age 12 when his father died, leaving his family in dire financial straights. Young Samuel found a job at the Hannibal Courier, and the meager food ration it paid helped the family survive. Three years later, at age 15, he became editor of the Hannibal Western Union and, by the time he was 21, Clemens earned good money and elevated social status as a licensed steamboat pilot on the Mississippi River.

The American Civil War ended his riverboat adventures and the money they paid. By 1961, Clemens lost everything and now eked out a meager living prospecting for gold in Nevada and points west.

Not for the first time in his life, Clemens found himself flat broke and in desperate of a job. He found work at the Virginia City Territorial Enterprise, where he pumped out stories with the distinct narrative style destined to become his calling card in Tom Sawyer and Huckleberry Finn. It was during this time he branded his work with his famous pen name, Mark Twain.

Late in his life both Oxford and Yale awarded him honorary degrees. Not bad for a kid who left school at 12 to help feed his family, driven by his passion and determination to succeed.

Maya Angelou

"You may not control all the events that happen to you, but you can decide not to be reduced by them. My mission in life is not merely to survive, but to thrive; and to do so with some passion, some compassion, some humor, and some style."

Live was never easy for Marguerite Annie Johnson. Her parents marriage ended when she was quite young and her father sent the children to live with his mother, Annie Henderson, in Stamps, Arkansas. They stayed there four years until her father showed up one day "without warning" and took the children back to St. Louis, where they once again lived with their mother.

It was here, at age 8, her mother's boyfriend raped young Marguerite. Her rapist faced trial, was convicted but served only a single day in jail. Four days after his release, her rapist was found dead. The common belief, never proven, was Angelou's uncles killed him for his crime. The entire ordeal so greatly traumatized her Maya Angelou stopped talking for almost five years. Her father sent her back to her grandmother's care, where she eventually started to speak again under the care of Bertha Flowers, who introduced the young girl to a wide variety of literary masterpieces.

Three weeks after completing her high school education, 17-year-old Marguerite Johnson gave birth to her son Clyde.

She changed her name to Maya Angelou at the urging of her manager at the Purple Onion, a San Francisco dance club where she performed nightly.

With her drive, passion and determination relentlessly propelling her forward, Maya Angelou transformed her life from child rape victim, fry cook, sex trade worker, nightclub dancer and singer to internationally renowned author. Her body of work includes articles, short stories, TV scripts, documentaries, autobiographies, and poetry. Her accomplishments still impact writers around the world to this day.

Agatha Christie

"Courage is the resolution to face the unforeseen."

Queen of Crime writer Agatha Christie, born Agatha Mary Clarissa Miller, is the world's second best-selling author of all time, behind only William Shakespeare.

She suffered from dyslexia, a learning disability making it difficult to spell and write, and dysgraphia, a handwriting impairment characterized by atrocious penmanship, and taking an unusually long time and great effort to write.

Christie's father died when she was just eleven years old, plunging her family into financial uncertainty. She was excruciatingly shy in front of strangers. Christie was home-schooled, and called herself the "slow one in the family." Nobody expected her to learn to read until she was eight years old.

None of this prevented Agatha Christie from selling over four billion copies of her 790 novels and dozens of short stories.

Sherrilyn Kenyon

"It's easy to look at people and make quick judgments about them, their present and their past, but you'd be amazed at the pain and tears a single smile hides. What a person shows to the world is only one tiny facet of the iceberg hidden from sight. And more often then not, it's lined with cracks and scars that go all the way to the foundation of their soul."

Sherrilyn Kenyon always knew she wanted to be a writer and she never doubted this destiny. An avid comic book fan, her dream was to work for Marvel, DC or DarkHorse. With a string of small successes under her belt, including her first professional sale at age 14, Kenyon applied to Georgia College with the ultimate goal of attending the University of Georgia's Creating Writing program. Due to her dyslexia, Kenyon's low placement test score landed her in a remedial English class instead.

She applied to University of Georgia's Creative Writing program three times and, on her third and final rejection, the admittance professor told her not to apply again, as the program was designed for students with talent and a serious future in publishing. Kenyon, he said, lacked both.

Discouraged, she tried switching her major to journalism. Her right hand is partially paralyzed, making it difficult to type. She failed the mandatory typing test.

Her older brother died when she was 20, leaving her bereft of her will to write. Three years later and married to her long-time boyfriend, she finally started writing again. Two years later she sold her first book, Born of Night. Kenyon published five more books before tragedy struck again. She almost died during the premature delivery of her son. The family lost everything due to medical expenses and lived out of their car in Columbus, MS.

The family worked their way back from their latest defeat and Kenyon continued to write. Stacks of rejection letters did not stop her and, in 1998 she finally found a publisher willing to take her on again. She successfully relaunched her writing career, never to be struck down again.

Sherrilyn Kenyon refused to allow personal tragedy, dyslexia, college rejection, publisher rejection or almost dying prevent her from achieving her dream.

She has sold over 70 million copies of her books in 100 countries. Her determination, self-discipline and will to succeed made it all possible.

Unstoppable Author

Stephen J. Cannell

"I don't struggle because I was always the stupidest kid in the class and the idea that I would ever be brilliant was knocked out of me in the third grade. So I'm not sitting around trying to be brilliant, or Shakespeare. I'm just trying to get the work I have in my head down on the page in the best way I possibly know how without putting that horrible pressure on myself of saying I'm going to write it today and in 200 years at Princeton they will be studying these words. Yeah, I want my stuff to be as good as I can conceivably make it, but I am not going to put that on my head."

Despite suffering from dyslexia, Stephen J. Cannell created almost 40 hit television series, including The Rockford Files, Baretta, Black Sheep Squadron, The A-Team, 21 Jump Street, Silk Stalkings and The Commish.

His undiagnosed dyslexia made it nearly impossible to do well in school. English was one of his most troubling courses. It was also his favourite and he proclaimed his ambition to become an author in his high school yearbook.

He succeeded beyond his own wildest dreams. His knowledge of his own limitations, combined with his self-discipline, drive and determination made his success inevitable.

Chapter 3

Daily Habits to Generate Success

Overview

This chapter covers the essential tasks every writer should practice each day to increase their output. You will find no earth-shattering bombshells here. You already know, intellectually, everything I'm about to tell you.

"So why bother reading this chapter?" you ask. To gain a deep emotional understanding of how these simple, common-sense activities will skyrocket your productivity and allow you to complete your book faster than you believe possible.

"Yeah, yeah," you say. "I've heard all this crap before. What can you possibly add that I don't already know?"

Perhaps nothing.

Perhaps everything.

I expose the multi-tasking lie and use a simple 3-minute test to prove single-tasking is the only way to achieve more in less time. Then I explain how to build new productivity habits fast, in three simple steps.

When you follow the course outlined ahead, you will transform your writing life.

You will write more words in less time.

You will write better words with less need to edit them later.

If this possibility holds no interest for you, close this book.

Go do something else.

If this possibility brings an eager, if somewhat disbelieving smile to your face, read on. You will believe soon enough.

If I can convince you, through sharing my own personal experience, how implementing these ideas will transform your creative life, I will take your bored thoughts of, "Yeah, I already know this," and transform them into "Wow, I want this level of productivity, too!"

Follow these three steps.

1. Design a daily productivity system.
2. Make the decision to implement your system.
3. Take the action required, every day and without exception, to execute your system.

It really is this simple.

A Daily Writing Routine is Necessary

In the second book in this series, Design Your Morning Routine: Jump-Start Your Daily Writing Success, I explained the necessity of a morning routine.

Willpower is a finite resource. We wake up with a specific amount of willpower and once its gone, our ability to make rational decisions falters, often in dramatic and unpleasant ways. Decision fatigue sets in. Our ability to remain focused on a single objective weakens. Our productivity drops like a stone, and we're left to wonder how it all went so horribly wrong, so fast.

When we automate the beginning of our day, we remove our need to make decisions. We keep our daily reserve of willpower topped up, ready for use when it counts most - throughout our work day.

The daily writing routine serves a similar purpose. When we work in a structured routine, we conserve our energy, our willpower, and our ability to make sound decisions so they are available to us when we need them most.

There is no magic to productivity, just correct planning, scheduling and execution. You might call it boring, and in one sense, it is.

The tortoise won the race by putting one foot in front of the other until he crossed the finish line. It doesn't get more boring than that.

At the end of each day, write a list of every task you must complete tomorrow. Rank them in order. When tomorrow starts, pull out your list and begin. When you decide what must be done first, ahead of time, you remove the hard decisions from the beginning of your work day. You work with greater focus and determination.

Simple, right?

Then why is it so difficult?

Self-discipline.

Self-discipline demands you take the path of most resistance, to go against your human nature. Self-discipline orders you to do what you know you should, when you should do it, whether you feel like it or not.

This is the path to success, whether your goal is to write a book, run a marathon, fly a plane, or move to Costa Rica and live on the beach.

To accomplish any of these worthy goals, you must sacrifice your time and energy today for a greater reward in the future.

You must delay gratification. You must pay the price to achieve success, the entire cost, not some small portion of it, and you must pay it up front, before you achieve your goal, before you know if you will be successful or not.

Building a Habit in Three Steps

Building a habit is a simple, three-step process best described as the Habit Loop by Charles Duhigg in his book *The Power of Habit: Why We Do What We Do in Life and Business*.

First, there is a cue, a trigger that instructs your brain to use a specific habit in automatic mode. Second, is the routine. This can be physical, mental or emotional. Third, is the reward that helps your brain decide if this particular habit loop is worth remembering in the future.

Over time, this loop—cue, routine, reward; cue, routine, reward—becomes more and more automatic. The cue and reward become intertwined until a powerful sense of anticipation and craving emerges.

Eventually, whether in a chilly MIT laboratory or your driveway, a habit is born.

The structure of the habit loop makes it easier to control. When you break a habit into its component parts, you can play with gear ratios, valve settings and tire pressure. You can experiment with habit loops to see which ones work best for you.

For example, my morning routine is a series of habit loops, strung together. Waking up is my cue to drink a glass of water. My routine is to walk to my desk and drink the 16 ounce glass of water I set out the night before. My reward is the knowledge water jump-starts my digestive system and hydrates my brain, which enables me to make better decisions.

Placing my empty water glass down on my desk is the cue to begin the next habit loop in the series. These habit loops allow me to complete every task required to start my day with a calm and focused mind - the foundation of a productive day.

Choose Responsibility, Don't Make Excuses

"Self-discipline is the ability to do what you should do, when you should do it, whether you feel like it or not."
—Elbert Hubbard

We twist ourselves in to pretzels to rationalize our way out of doing what we know we must do, when we must do it. Those mental gymnastics reveal our lack of self-discipline. The first step to writing your book (yes, I know I have dozens of "first steps") is to take full responsibility for your progress.

In his book No Excuses! The Power of Self-Discipline, author Brian Tracy exhorts readers to either do something or don't, but stop making excuses for your lack of action.

> No more excuses! Do it or don't do it—but don't make excuses. Stop using your incredible brain to think up elaborate rationalizations and justifications for not taking action. Do something. Do anything. Get on with it! Repeat to yourself: "If it's to be, it's up to me!"

Losers make excuses; winners make progress. Now, how can you tell if your favorite excuse is valid or not? It's simple. Look around and ask, "Is there anyone else who has my same excuse who is successful anyway?" When you ask this question, if you are honest, you will have to admit that there are thousands and even millions of people who have had it far worse than you who have gone on to do wonderful things with their lives. And what thousands and millions of others have done, you can do as well—if you try.

If we put half as much energy into finishing our book as we put into avoiding it, if we stopped making excuses for why we can't write, we would churn out a book a month for the rest of our lives.

If I could do what is in front of me to do, instead of making excuses for why I won't do it, I would be far more productive and far happier. On any given day, I spend twice as much time avoiding my job as I spend writing. (The ratio is probably three or four to one, but that much self-honesty is too hard to face.)

The next time you procrastinate when you know you should write, don't make an excuse. Take responsibility for the decision you made, and figure out how to make a different choice. For me, this always starts with making a different choice **right now**.

Open up your writing timer, hit the start button and write.

Yes, it is this easy and this hard, for me. I suspect your mileage is the same... if you are honest with yourself.

But you already know you can achieve any goal you desire if you exercise self-discipline and don't quit until you're done, don't you?

The Power of Self-Discipline

"Discipline is the bridge between goals and accomplishment."
—Jim Rohn

Webster's Dictionary defines self-discipline as "correction or regulation of oneself for the sake of improvement." Whether we label it self-discipline, self-control, self-denial or delayed gratification, our achievements and our successes are the end result of the actions we take.

Authors share a common trait. We don't want to do the things we know we should do to achieve success.

This is true for both successful authors and unpublished writers.

Successful authors employ self-discipline. They take the actions required to accomplish their goals when they would rather do something else, something more fun, in the short term. Their willingness to delay gratification is the key embodied in the phrase short term pain for long term gain.

Brian Tracy, in his book No Excuses!, discusses how our character is defined by our willingness to take those actions necessary to ensure our success, even when we don't want to.

> The only bulwark against temptation, the path of least resistance, and the expediency factor is character. The only way that you can develop your full character is by exerting your willpower in every situation when you are tempted to do what is easy and expedient rather than what is correct and necessary.[6]

Proper systems, such as a pre-determined structure for our work day ensures our success, with one important caveat - we must implement the plan contained within this structure. What separates successful authors from others is their ability to do what they should do, when they should do it, whether they feel like it or not.

Do I want to write for four hours every day? If I judge my results by this week, my answer is a resounding "NO!"

I would rather do anything else. I also know my current work in progress, the book you now hold in your hands, cannot write itself. Despite my own struggles with procrastination and self-discipline, I write every day because I also understand the immense satisfaction that awaits me when this book is finished.

This victory lap at the end of Publication Highway is my objective. Only when I delay my gratification in the short term is this victory lap possible.

My editor views me as a highly productive writer. My own view differs, by orders of magnitude.

Nicolas only sees the finished projects as they land on his desk. I see what he does not - my daily struggle to do the things I know I must do, when I must do them, whether I want to or not.

I also anticipate the joy when a fellow author, perhaps you, writes to tell me how this book changed their life and helped them complete their book faster than they ever imagined possible.

Those feelings of happiness, joy and satisfaction are only possible if I mercilessly employ self-discipline to get the job done.

So far, it's working.

Action is a Reflection of Your Commitment to Achieve Your Goal

Make a decision. Follow it with action.

Those seven words are the mantra for my life. It drives my wife crazy every time I say it, although she understands the power these ten words wield in my life.

Success in means we must make rational decisions and follow those good decisions with correct action. Writing a book is no different.

The actions you take (or don't take) reveal your level of commitment. If you do not write every day, you will despise this thought. If you do write every day, if only for 15 minutes, you will nod your head in agreement and ask what you can cut from your life to double your daily writing time.

Action equals commitment.

Lack of action? You got it. Lack of commitment.

Make a decision. Follow it with action. Immediately.

Tomorrow is too late.

Write Your Goals Down Daily

If self-discipline is the key to success in life, clarity is the lock it opens.

The more often you write your goals down on paper, the clearer they become.

Each day before you begin work, place a blank sheet of paper in front of you and write out all your goals. Do this every morning, without exception. Train yourself to complete this one vital task.

This habit will take you three minutes per day, at most. The impact upon your life, however, is immense. Clarity brings power to your life. Clarity allows your subconscious mind to devote its resources to solving the challenges you face. Your life will improve. Resources you didn't even know you need will show up when you need them. You will make more progress toward your goals in less and less time.

Ultimately, writing down your goals every morning is a test. It's a testament to your determination, your self-discipline and your desire to achieve.

This exercise in self-discipline is part of the price you must pay for success.

If you find this is difficult, at first, do not fear. Persevere. If you struggle against your own internal resistance, uncover what causes it and resolve the issue. For me, it feels like I'm afraid my dreams might come true and I'll accomplish the outlandish goals I set, which means I have a lot more work to do around my own fear of success.

Daily, Dedicated Writing Time is Essential

This book teaches you to design and implement systems to uphold your desire to write. The foundation of this system is to schedule specific time slots in your day to write. The more time you write each day, specifically the more words you write per day, determines how long you will take to complete your book. Simply put, the more time you write, the more words you will put on the page.

The most important part of your day are the precious minutes you dedicate to writing, with no interruption. No matter what else you do each day, you must find a way to schedule time to write, even if it's only for 15 minutes.

Daily Physical Exercise

If you already incorporate exercise into your Morning Routine, you can skip this section. If you do not exercise each morning, please begin immediately. The increased focus you derive from daily exercise must be experienced to be believed.

Billionaire Richard Branson says working out significantly boosts his productivity.[7] He credits his 5am daily workout habit as the foundation of his own morning routine. His belief is backed by science.

When you work out, your brain releases a chemical called brain-derived neurotrophic factor (BDNF), which improves brain function.

According to MakeYourBodyWork.com[8] there are seven primary benefits to a morning workout.

1. It enhances your metabolism.

When you exercise in the morning you burn more calories later in the day, after you stop exercising, compared to those who do not exercise at all. You benefit from exercise once, when you work out, and again after you stop. Bonus points for doubling your benefits.

2. It cultivates a mindset of consistency.

In other words, it builds a positive habit.

When you eat this frog first, you never miss a workout because you're "too busy."

3. It improves your physical and mental energy levels.

It is impossible to walk and be depressed at the same time. Morning exercise helps you set a positive mindset, regardless of your mood when you begin your workout.

4. It builds self-discipline.

As with most habits, exercise in the morning gets easier with time.

5. You sleep better.

This claim is backed up research, according to Dr. Scott Collier[10], assistant professor in the Department of Health, Leisure and Exercise Science in Appalachian's College of Health Sciences.

In every case, those who exercised at 7 a.m. experienced roughly a 10 percent reduction in blood pressure, a reduction they carried through the rest of the day. Their blood pressure also dipped about 25 percent at night, they slept longer, with more beneficial sleep cycles than when they exercised at other times of the day.

6. Helps you achieve your fitness goals.

When you wake up early to exercise and fore-go an extra 30 minutes of sleep, you are more determined to reap the reward for your sacrifice. This increases your personal determination to achieve your other goals as well.

7. Improves your love life.

Trainer Dave Smith asks, "Do I even need to argue this one? You have created a strong habit of morning exercise, your metabolism is flowing, your body is looking and feeling better, you're sleeping well at night, and your mind is as sharp as ever. Are you enjoying your new life yet?"

He makes a valid point.

Try it.

Clean Up Your Workspace

A cluttered desk reflects a cluttered mind. Conversely, an organized desk reflects an organized mind.

Those two thoughts terrify me, and for good reason. As any photograph of my office taken in the past 20 years proves, it's a daily challenge to keep my desk from turning into a garbage dump.

Do I feel better when my desk is clean and uncluttered? Absolutely. This positive emotion isn't enough to motivate me to keep my desk clean, unfortunately.

My struggle with desk clutter continues.

I want to publish a photograph of my desk to my Twitter account each morning as an accountability measure. Yes, the thought of doing this scares the daylights out of me. My fear means I should publish one of those photos today and repeat this public shaming until my behavior improves.

That's what I call a serious reason to procrastinate.

Read for One Hour Every Day

We all wake up with the same 1,440 minutes per day.

The difference between the successful, published author and the writer with the unfinished manuscript is choice. The successful, published author makes a conscious decision to spend those valuable minutes in pursuit of the most important tasks in his or her day.

If you want to write, you must read every day.

Stephen King's words on this subject are almost Biblical.

> "If you don't have time to read, you don't have the time (or the tools) to write. Simple as that."

Studies of successful business people confirm this is true, and not only for writers.

Brian Tracy explains the value of reading, no matter what you do for a living.

> "If you read only one book per month, that will put you into the top 1% of income earners in our society. But if you read one book per week, 50 books per year, that will make you one of the best educated, smartest, most capable and highest paid people in your field. Regular reading will transform your life completely."

Before you complain you don't have time to read for an hour each day, ask yourself, will you really miss your third hour in front of the television tonight? Or even your second?

Set aside one hour per day to read. Make this a priority, a commitment you must keep, no matter what else happens in your day. Television might be nice, enjoyable even, but your favorite TV show is not essential to your success. Reading is, both as a writer and as a human being.

Choose one activity you can do less or eliminate entirely to make space for reading.

I break my daily reading commitment into two 30-minute sessions. I read a book about writing craft to enhance my skills in the first session.

For the second half hour, I read a book in my chosen genre to develop a sense of what good and bad writing looks like. This is an excellent way to improve my own skills. I also experience, first-hand, what other authors are writing in my genre so I don't add their overused ideas into my work through sheer ignorance. That would be embarrassing.

Reading also improves my self-editing skills. The awareness raised by reading their work shows me the pitfalls I must avoid in mine. It also teaches me how to write cleaner, more effective prose.

Make the choice to read for one hour every day. Develop this habit and at the end of one year, reflect on how this single choice enhanced your skill as a writer.

The Power of No

The single greatest skill you can develop is your ability to say "No." This is critical when you start to make changes to your daily routine.

Your "No" unleashes the three-headed monster in everyone close to you, called Resistance to Change.

It forces your loved ones to view you in a new way, to find different ways to interact with you and adapt to your new focus. They won't like it. Not even when they tell you how great it is you're finally writing the book you always wanted to write. At least, not at first. They will test you to make sure you are serious, to see whether this is another half-hearted attempt or whether you are truly committed to your new path.

"No" is your greatest ally in this battle. For added effect, follow it with the words "And please close the door of my office behind you."

Be polite, but don't be surprised if you find yourself on the receiving end of a few dagger-filled glares. This is perfectly normal behavior, and subsides as soon as you prove your commitment, both to yourself and to them.

Do not forget the flip side of your "No." You must make time for your loved ones after of your writing session if you expect them to remain your loved ones.

Start Your Day With A Golden or Power Hour

The only difference between Brian Tracy's Golden Hour and Anthony Robbins' Power Hour is the name. Both men recommend you ignore all electronic devices for the first hour of your work day. No email, no Facebook, no Twitter, no text messages.

They also recommend you write a gratitude list. A daily gratitude list accomplishes two important goals - it humbles your mind and delivers a list of people, events and things we're grateful for. Reflect on your list for a few minutes and focus on your gratitude for each person on it.

For the next five minutes, focus on what you will be grateful for when it manifests in your life. These are the things you desire, but have not yet achieved. Focus on these goals like you have already achieved them. Express your gratitude for receiving them.

With your feet firmly planted in humility and gratitude, you can move forward to accomplish any goal you focus your mind on.

Write out each individual task you must accomplish today. Be specific. Your hardest task belongs at the top of the list. When you are done, reflect on your list for a minute.

Are the items in the correct order?

Can any item on your list wait? If so, remove it.

Is something missing? If so, add it to your list in the appropriate space.

Eat your frog.

Do the single hardest task of your work day first. Do the one thing you least want to do, the one thing that will impact your future success the greatest. We all have at least one frog. For me, today, it's writing this book. Nothing more important today than finishing this book.

Write out your goals for the year. When you write out your long-term goals every day, you tell your subconscious mind what is important. You give your subconscious mind its marching orders, then leave it alone to do what it does best - solve the problem of how to achieve your goals.

Spend ten minutes to reflect on your long-term goals.

Are they still valid?

If you receive "No" for an answer and continue to receive "No" for a week or more, perhaps it is time to re-evaluate your decision.

Chapter 4
The Great Multi-Tasking Lie

The Thief of Time

The biggest time thief in your life is the lie of multi-tasking. If you believe you are more effective when you do two things at once, you deceive yourself.

The human mind can focus on one primary task at a time.

Now, before you tell me you multi-task all the time, remember my qualifier of one **primary** task. Sure, you can talk on the phone and walk across the room. You can chew bubblegum and skip down the street, if that's your thing, but you cannot drive and read your Facebook feed simultaneously without disastrous consequences.

Likewise, you cannot write a book and watch television at the same time. Sure, your computer is on and your word processor is open, but you are either engrossed in the story unfolding before your eyes on the television or writing your book while you ignore the stupid box.

There is no middle ground.

Dave Crenshaw, a leading productivity and leadership coach, created a test to prove multi-tasking or task-switching is ineffective.

In his humorous and educational video, he asks the viewer to grab a piece of paper and a pen, and take his multi-tasking test, which I've modified slightly.

1. Draw four horizontal lines on the page.

2. Time yourself writing the words "Multi-Tasking is a liar and a thief" on the first line, and the numbers 1 thru 36 on the second line. Note how long it took to complete this task.

3. Time yourself again, only this time, write the first letter of the phrase on the third line, followed by the first number on the fourth line. Repeat this process of writing one letter and one number per line until you spell out the phrase "Multi-Tasking is a liar and a thief" on the third line and the numbers 1 thru 36 on the fourth line.

This exercise takes five minutes to complete, at most, but will transform your view of multi-tasking (or task-switching) forever.

The disastrous consequences of multi-tasking are:

- ❑ Your work takes longer to complete,
- ❑ Your work contains more errors, and
- ❑ your stress level increases.

All three negatively impact your productivity.

View his amusing and educational video on YouTube:

https://youtu.be/BCeGKxz3Q8Q

Chapter 5
Apply Self-Honesty

Introduction

Complete the following exercises with total honesty. You gain points for truth and self-knowledge, not denial and self-delusion. The entire process takes less than one hour. The result will change your life.

Grab a notepad and pen, and let's begin.

Self-Honesty Begins With A List

All great things begin with a list, and this exercise is no different.

What must you do each day?

This includes work, walking the dog, and spending time with your family. Include how long you watch television, spend on Twitter, Facebook and other social media sites, hang out on your smart phone, coffee with friends, work, family time not spent glued to the idiot box, and the daily commute to and from your job.

Write out a comprehensive list of your daily activities. Beside each item on the list, write down how much time you spend on that activity.

Do this for seven days. At the end of seven days, add up the totals for each column.

Here's the terrible truth. The activity with the highest number is what you value most. You may say you don't value work even though you spend most of your time there. I respectfully disagree. Whether you like work or not is irrelevant. I didn't ask for a list of what you liked most. I asked what activities you spent your time on.

If you spend the majority of your time on work, you value it above everything else in your life. Why? It meets one or more of your six core needs.

Yes, this is difficult. I hated this process the first dozen times I completed it, too. Eventually, as I changed my life to focus on what is important, the numbers attached to each item began to shift.

You must start with the truth - where you are right now - before you can change anything.

Grab your notebook or, better yet, download the worksheet I created for you and print a copy. Then be honest with yourself for the next seven days. It's worth it. I promise.

https://ChristopherDiArmani.net/free-daily-routine-workbook

7-Day Evaluation

In the previous exercise, you wrote down everything you must do each day, for an entire week.

With those pages as your guide, write out each item in a logical sequence, along with your estimated time to complete each task.

Can you reduce how much time you spend on any of these activities?

Is there anything you can delete from the list entirely?

Examine your list again.

Where can you squeeze out 15 minutes to write?

Are there two or three times in your day you could do this?

After careful consideration of these thoughts, set these pages aside.

Come back to them after you complete the rest of this section, when you will use them to construct the first draft of your daily writing routine.

What Is Your Biggest Dream?

Write down your dreams for your writing life, whatever they may be.

Do you want to become a famous author? Do you want to write 100 books before you die? Do you want to fly to Mars? Whatever your dreams, write them down. If your list feels too long, don't worry. That's normal. Most people have far more dreams than they realize until they write them down.

When you're finished, examine your list. Rewrite your list on a separate page, ranked in order of priority, from your most-desired goal to your least.

What heads the list? Is the order correct? Don't answer right away. You can always revisit your thoughts later.

Remember, there are no right or wrong answers. These are your dreams, so embrace the process and be diligent. No dream is too silly or too inconsequential. If it enters your mind, write it down.

What Are You Passionate About?

The things you are most passionate about are the same things you desire with all your heart. Think about your life, your past accomplishments, and list every activity or idea you are enthusiastic about.

For example, I'm passionate about learning. and I'm passionate about sharing my self-improvement discoveries with others. It's why I wrote this series. This joy, this passion, drove me to write and publish an entire series in less time than it takes most people to write their first draft of a single book.

Write down everything you are passionate about. Nothing is off limits. No area of your life is out of bounds.

Rank your passions in order from most intense to least. What does this list reveal to you? Write those conclusions down as well.

What Core Needs Drive You?

To determine which core needs drive you to write, you must uncover which of your needs are met by writing and publishing a book. When you understand which core needs you meet by writing, designing a daily routine to meet those needs becomes a no-brainer.

The first link is a 10-question survey from Tony Robbins and, in my experience, gives a surprisingly accurate overview.

http://core.tonyrobbins.com/driving-force-2/human-needs/builder - 99WT-207FX.html

The second questionnaire is longer, designed to give a greater level of accuracy and detail.

http://six-human-needs-test.herokuapp.com/members/new

This is the online version of a physical questionnaire originally designed by Cloe Madanes, and if you prefer, you can download a PDF version of the test from the bottom of this page:

http://www.shelleyhannafineart.com/how-to-find-out-what-you-really-need/

Complete one or both of these questionnaires.

Their results offer knowledge and insight into how your mind works and which core needs most influence your decision-making processes, both conscious and sub-conscious. Then you can make informed decisions about your most effective path forward.

What Do You Want To Write?

In a few sentences, explain what your book is about and why it is important for you to write it.

Next, write down why you are the best person to write it, if not the only person who can write it.

How Much Time Do You Write Each Day?

How many hours do you write each day? This is not an exercise in personal shaming, but in truth and self-honesty. The goal is to be brutally honest with yourself so you can improve. So, what's your number? Write it down. Stare at it on the page in front of you. How do you feel? Write down your emotional response. Track how this emotional reaction changes over the next 60 days as you devote more of your time to writing.

What Is Your Current Writing Speed?

No matter how many words you write per hour today, you cannot learn to write faster without some basic information. If you want to write faster and be more productive, follow the exercise below to determine your baseline.

This is way more fun than it sounds, honest!

Set your writing timer for 15 minutes. Why 15? Why not 10 minutes? Or 5? Because my own experience with this test produced strange results. I cannot explain how or why, but with the timer set for 15 minutes, I write twice as many words as when the timer is set for 10 minutes. You're right. It makes no sense. None whatsoever. Yet no matter how often I run the test, my results are the same.

If you don't have a smart phone app, try these alternatives:

https://tomato-timer.com/

https://ChristopherDiArmani.net/free-pomodoro-writing-timer

Start the timer.

Write for 15 minutes, uninterrupted. It doesn't matter what you write, so long as you write until the timer expires.

At the end of the 15 minutes, take note of your word count. Write it down in your notebook. This is your baseline.

Run this test three or four times to see what, if anything, changes when you use different writing prompts. Odds are good you will write about the same number of words each time, but if there is a wide disparity, see if you can pin down what's causing it.

No, you cannot skip this step. It's the bedrock upon which you build your writing productivity plan.

Writing Prompts

If you need a writing prompt for this exercise, choose one from the list on the next page, or use one of the online writing prompt generators listed in the Resources chapter at the end of the book.

1. You discover your friend harbors a secret.
2. Someone stabs you in your dreams. You wake up to discover it wasn't a dream.
3. You overheard a conversation and can't get it out of your mind.
4. Describe meeting your greatest love.
5. What is the one thing you cannot live without?
6. The garden was overgrown now.
7. What did the last person to praise you say?
8. Describe the most fragile object you held in your hands.
9. Describe your worst sports nightmare.
10. You wake up to the sound of a dog barking.

When Do You Want Your Book Completed?

If you could finish your book on any date, when would you do so?

Be specific. Decide upon a single calendar day, month and year and write it down.

Does The Math Work?

First, if your current daily word count is small, do not allow this number to prevent you from writing your book. No writer in history ever picked up a pen for the first time and wrote 2,000 words a day. We all started the same way - writing the words we could each day - and improved our daily output over time.

> Do not despise these small beginnings, for the LORD rejoices to see the work begin…
>
> — Zechariah 4:10 (*The Bible, New Living Translation, 2nd Edition*)

Second, each genre has different recommended word counts and, even then, the correct length for your book will vary with every person you ask. Chuck Sambuchino, in his WritersDigest.com article *Word Count for Novels and Children's Books: The Definitive Post*,[12] says,

> Between 80,000 and 89,999 words is a good range you should be aiming for. This is a 100% safe range for literary, mainstream, women's, romance, mystery, suspense, thriller and horror. Anything in this word count won't scare off any agent anywhere.

Is your proposed deadline realistic based on your current daily word count? Here's how to know, for sure.

You must write 80,000 words to complete your book, using the low end of Sambuchino's range. How long it takes to write the words is up to you. You can write as fast or as slow as you like, but you are not finished until you write all 80,000 words. The determining factor, the number of words you write each day, is completely under your control.

To determine how many days you need to write your book, use the formula TWR / WPD = N, where

TWR = Total Words Required to complete your book.
WPD = How many Words you write Per Day.
N = Number of days required to complete your book.

For example:

80,000 / 300 words per day = 267 days to complete your book.
80,000 / 500 words per day = 160 days to complete your book.
80,000 / 1,000 words per day = 80 days to complete your book.

Double your daily word count and cut the time it takes to write your first draft in half.

80,000 / 2,000 words per day = 40 days to complete your book.

Increase your output again by just 50% and you can write an entire first draft in a single month.

80,000 / 3,000 words per day = 27 days to complete your book.

You can take as many years as you want to write your book, but there is no unwritten rule saying you must take a long time.

Here is a small sampling of famous books and their word counts:[13]

1. The Color Purple by Alice Walker - 66,556
2. The Sun Also Rises by Ernest Hemingway - 67,707
3. Crime and Punishment by Fyodor Dostoyevsky - 211,591
4. Walden by Henry David Thoreau - 114,634
5. Slaughterhouse-Five by Kurt Vonnegut - 49,459
6. The Adventures of Huck Finn by Mark Twain - 109,571
7. The Picture of Dorian Gray by Oscar Wilde - 78,462
8. Fahrenheit 451 by Ray Bradbury - 46,118
9. The Martian Chronicles by Ray Bradbury - 64,768
10. War and Peace by Leo Tolstoy - 587,287

Chapter 6

Take Action

Are You Committed to Writing Your Book?

One of my favorite movies of all time is Boondock Saints, written by Troy Duffy, starring Sean Patrick Flanery, Norman Reedus and Billy Connolly.

Near the end of the movie, Connolly, the father, responds to a question from his eldest son, played by Sean Patrick Flanery.

Connor looks to his father.

"How far are we going with this, Da?" he asks.

His father leans forward into the light.

"The question is not, 'how far?' The question is, 'Do you possess the constitution, the depth of faith to go as far as is needed?'"

It's an awesome scene and presents a fundamental question every author must answer.

The question is not "How long will it take to write my book?"

The question is, "Do I possess the constitution, the depth of character and the self-discipline to write 1,000 words every day, every single day no matter what, until my book is complete?"

Since you're still here, reading this page, my fervent prayer is that you answered with a resounding "Yes!"

Construct Your Daily Writing Routine

Grab the pages from your 7-day evaluation of your life, the ones I asked you to set aside earlier, and spread them out in front of you.

Examine the pages and cross off everything not relevant to earning a paycheck, time with your family, and writing. These are the necessities of your daily life.

Write out the list of every action you must take each day.

Beside each item, write down your time estimate for each one. When you're finished, take a break. You've earned it.

Build Your Daily Plan for Success

In the previous exercises you wrote down everything you must do in the course of your day. With this list as your guide, write out each item in a logical sequence, along with your estimated time to complete each task.

In the companion workbook is a sample Writing Productivity Planner sheet, and seven blank planner templates. Take a look at the sample and then construct your daily work and writing schedule.

Your Daily Writing Routine is a Work In Progress

Field Marshal Helmuth Karl Bernhard Graf von Moltke, Chief of Staff for the Prussian Army, was a tactical genius, yet he is remembered more for his thoughts on planning than any battlefield victory.

"No battle plan ever survives contact with the enemy."

Your daily routine will always be a work in progress, something to refine again and again. It will never be etched in stone.

Its purpose is to provide structure to your day, to schedule those tasks you know you must complete, no matter what else happens.

Events will occur beyond your ability to foresee. Such is life. Deal with them as needed and get back to your schedule as soon as possible.

Congratulations!

You did it! You created your daily writing routine.

Now it's time to apply self-discipline to achieve your goals.

For me, this is a daily battle.

At heart, I'm lazy. I love writing but I want the *easy* road to publication. I don't want to do the hard work of writing every day. The daily routine is B-O-R-I-N-G.

Here's the thing. It's also the easiest, fastest and most effective way to finish and publish my book. I also discovered I am far happier when I follow the structure of my daily routine. I write more words, better words, faster than any other time in my life.

I didn't build this system because I was bored one day. I built it because I knew, through my own pain, suffering and failure, I needed to change the way I wrote if I was to ever finish my book.

Seven books and four workbooks published in three months is a pretty incredible accomplishment, and one I could never achieve without my daily routine and personal writing productivity system.

My fervent prayer is you will take the same leap of faith I did and join me on a pilgrimage down Publication Highway. It's an amazing journey and one you do not want to miss!

Download the Free Workbook

The Plan for Success is Written on Paper

Research by Dr. Gail Matthews[14] at the Dominican University of California confirmed the mythical and never-performed but often-cited Harvard or Yale study on the power of written goals.

The mythical study claimed only 3% of the graduating class wrote down their goals and 20 years later out-earned their classmates by over ten times.

While not quite so earth-shattering as an exponential earning power, Dr. Matthews' study confirms when you write down your goals you are more likely to follow through and achieve them.

The action of writing down your personal goals increases your likelihood to follow through on your commitment, to take the actions required to achieve your goals.

Pretty simple, right? Obvious, even, yet so many people do not write down their goals, decreasing their chances for success. That's plain crazy.

This is also true for your daily activities. If you do not plan for success, if you do not schedule time to write and keep the appointment, you will not write. Your own experience proves this true, doesn't it?

Download your free PDF copy of the Prolific Author Workbook.

Complete every exercise to build your daily plan for success.

Your published book depends upon it.

https://ChristopherDiArmani.net/free-prolific-author-workbook

The Road to Writing Success is Finishing Your Book

The seven keys to writing success are:

1. Self-honesty
2. Clearly defined goals
3. Be committed to achieving your goal
4. Apply self-discipline
5. Be consistent
6. Be persistent
7. Be accountable

You cannot publish what you do not complete and done is better than perfect. Your book will never be perfect. Accept that truth and move on.

Learn the tips and tricks to complete your manuscript easier, faster and better that you ever thought possible.

Join me on the incredible journey down Publication Highway.

Read the fifth book in the Author Success Foundations series, *Done is Better Than Perfect - Seven Keys to Finish Writing Your Book Fast* to learn how perfectionism kills dreams and finishing is always better than failure. Learn the secret of Getting to Done.

Available from your favorite online book retailers today.

For more information, visit:

https://ChristopherDiArmani.net/DoneIsBetter

One Last Thing!

First, thank you for reading this book!

If you enjoyed this book and found it informative (and even if you did not) I would be grateful if you would post an honest review on Amazon and/or Goodreads. Every review helps this book find more readers, the lifeblood of any author.

http://ChristopherDiArmani.net/Review-

http://ChristopherDiArmani.net/Review-

Your support in the form of an honest review really does make a difference. Reviews help authors sell more books and I read every one as part of my efforts to make my books even better.

I would also be grateful if you shared a link to this book on your social media accounts.

If, for some reason, you did not like this book or didn't get what you expected out of it please tell me directly. I will use your constructive criticism to fix any flaws in my book so it better meets your expectations. Please contact me here:

https://ChristopherDiArmani.net/Contact

Thank you so much for your support, feedback and your honest reviews.

Sincerely,

Christopher di Armani

Author Extraordinare

http://ChristopherDiArmani.net/Books

About Christopher di Armani

"Author Extraordinaire"

Christopher di Armani is an Amazon bestselling author and the creator of Author Success Foundations.

This 7-book series teaches authors at any level how to develop the mindset, daily routines and work habits necessary to unleash their creativity and get their books published.

He has published 16 books and produced 4 documentary films on topics ranging from the craft of writing to civil liberties and politics.

Download your free introduction to the Author Success Foundations series at

https://ChristopherDiArmani.net/AuthorSuccessFoundations

Books by Christopher

Awaken Your Author Mindset: Finish Writing Your Book Fast (Author Success Foundations 1)

https://ChristopherDiArmani.net/author-mindset

https://ChristopherDiArmani.net/author-mindset-workbook

Learn how to develop your bullet-proof Author Mindset and create a system guaranteed to deliver success and to build the habits required to work this system every single day.

The choice is yours. If you continue to do what you've always done you'll just get what you already have, an unfinished manuscript and all the disappointment, discarded dreams and self-loathing you can handle.

You will never finish your book.

Now, imagine the possible…

Allow me to be your guide to help you construct a mindset, a solid foundation to complete your manuscript so published becomes, not just possible, but inevitable. This is the power of the Author Mindset.

Design Your Morning Routine: Jump-Start Your Writing Success (Author Success Foundations Book 2)

https://ChristopherDiArmani.net/morning-routine

https://ChristopherDiArmani.net/morning-routine-workbook

There is no magic to writing a book. None. You take action, every single day, until your book is finished. You plan, schedule and execute the plan. You write.

If you are serious about finishing your manuscript, grab your notebook, a pen, and a cup of your favorite beverage, and join me at the kitchen table. We'll chat about habits, willpower and self-discipline. We'll discuss how the mind functions, what makes a habit stick, and how our willpower fades throughout the day. We'll talk about concrete steps to improve your self-discipline.

Then I'll ask you to complete a series of exercises. These exercises reveal, at a deep level, what's important to you - what you value most in life. This clarity of purpose allows you to create a morning routine designed to jump-start your daily writing output.

Author Focus: Develop Your Author Vision Statement and Laser-Focus Your Writing Career (Author Success Foundations Book 3)

https://ChristopherDiArmani.net/author-focus

https://ChristopherDiArmani.net/author-focus-workbook

Writing is easy. Finishing your book is easy, too.

Focus. Be diligent. Apply self-discipline and determination.

You already possess these qualities. This book would not appeal to you if you didn't.

Your author vision statement is an extraordinary targeting mechanism to guide you to your ultimate destination - the end of Publication Highway.

The exercises ahead serve one purpose - to focus your mind on what you value most - your published book.

Join me and map your personal journey down Publication Highway. Discover what you value most, not just in writing, but in your entire life.

Isn't your ideal future worth the time?

Prolific Author: The Step-by-Step Guide to Write More Words in Less Time and Finish Your Book Fast (Author Success Foundations 4)

https://ChristopherDiArmani.net/prolific-author

https://ChristopherDiArmani.net/prolific-author-workbook

The key to unlock your drive to succeed is knowing why you write. When you understand how your desire to write fulfills your core needs, you transform writing from a chore to be dreaded into the vision you were born to fulfill. Time set aside to write becomes as critical to your life as the food you eat and the water you drink.

If we believe success does not matter, neither does the road we travel to get there.

Success matters. The road you travel to achieve success matters more.

Your daily writing routine is the last piece of the puzzle to build a life focused on accomplishing your goal - a finished and published book.

Done is Better than Perfect: 7 Keys to Finish Writing Your Book Fast (Author Success Foundations 5)

https://ChristopherDiArmani.net/DoneIsBetter

Give Up Your Perfectionism and Publish Your Book

The three fundamental truths of writing are:

1. Your book will never be perfect.
2. You cannot publish what you do not complete.
3. Done is better than perfect.

Learn how to finish your book easier, faster and better than you ever thought possible when you apply the Seven Keys of Writing Success.

Become Unstoppable: 7 Habits of Highly Successful Authors (Author Success Foundations Book 6)

https://ChristopherDiArmani.net/become-unstoppable

Success leaves clues.

Figure out what successful authors did to advance their careers, then do what they did. It's the most effective course of action. Simple concept, but we must do the work. You know, the hard part.

In the pages ahead I discuss how each habit works, as well as the lies we tell ourselves to rationalize our lack of forward progress. Finally, I shine the light of truth on the lies we tell ourselves and watch as they scurry away like little cockroaches.

Apply these principles to your life and you'll achieve their success. It's inevitable. All it takes is a pinch of perseverance, a dash of focus, and two cups of hard work.

I Don't Have Time To Write And Other Lies Writers Tell Themselves (Author Success Foundations Book 7)

https://ChristopherDiArmani.net/no-time-to-write

Stop Lying To Yourself.

In this installment of the Author Success Foundations series, I dissect seven lies writers tell ourselves and shine the light of truth upon each one.

Every falsehood obscures a truth we refuse to confront. The job of a writer, any writer, is to face our fears head on, protected by the body armor of honesty and integrity. Only then does the brilliance we etch on the page shine bright for the world to see.

Each delusion corrodes holes in our armor, holes the insidious demons of worry, self-doubt, procrastination and perfectionism slip through to poison us.

The Author Success Foundations series provides the tools and materials to patch those holes, to reinforce and strengthen our armor. The day of battle is here, and we must march ever forward. If we stop, even for a moment, our words shrink under the oppressive heat of our fears and we fail.

Step inside. Face your fears. Show these pathetic demons you cannot be cowed. Own your internal dialog and reshape it into a powerful engine, then use that power to drive down Publication Highway.

The Simple 3-Step Secret to Slaughter Writer's Block And Vanquish it Forever

https://ChristopherDiArmani.net/Writers-Block-Book

There is no more perfect Hell than one where I cannot write. You know that terror, too, don't you? That sense your last remaining creative spark abandoned you some time back. It's sickening.

Let me show you how to extricate yourself from that "perfect Hell" permanently.

TOP SECRET - Inspiration, Motivation and Encouragement - 701 Essential Quotes for Writers

https://ChristopherDiArmani.net/Top-Secret-Quotes

This compilation of 701 quotes delivers inspiration, motivation and encouragement on 39 aspects of writing and the writing life.

You will discover quotes to make you laugh and quotes to make you cry. Some are familiar, like old friends. Others you will meet for the first time. All have a common theme: The Writing Life.

When you need it most, you will find words of encouragement here.

Filming Police is Legal - How to Hold Police Accountable While Staying Out of Jail

I write about police issues regularly. I highlight good cops when I can, but I focus on the problems in our police forces with honesty, integrity and abuse. Every time news breaks about police seizing another citizen's camera or cell phone I receive the same question.

Christopher, is it legal to film police?

The unequivocal answer is a court-affirmed YES. It is legal to film police in every state in the United States of America and in every single province and territory of Canada. That YES comes with specific caveats for the audio portion of a recording depending upon your jurisdiction, and it is critical you know those caveats.

The purpose of this book is to educate mere citizens and police forces alike about the legality of the right of citizens to film police, along with an examination of the legal history supporting our legal right to do so.

https://ChristopherDiArmani.net/Filming-Police

Justin Trudeau - 47 Character-Revealing Quotes from Canada's 23rd Prime Minister and What They Mean for You

On October 19, 2015 Canadians elected their 23rd Prime Minister based on good looks, nice hair and a famous name.

They voted for style over substance.

Our 23rd Prime Minister's entire leadership experience consisted of teaching snowboarding lessons and high school drama. His management experience consisted of administering his trust fund and his ego.

Not a single thought was given to what he stood for, what his party stood for, or what he would actually do once elected to the highest office in the land. That bothered me. That bothered me so much I began to research his much-publicized missteps and that in turn revealed a disturbing pattern within Trudeau's numerous faux pas. That pattern is the focus of this book.

https://ChristopherDiArmani.net/Justin-Trudeau-Book-1

From Refugee to Cabinet Minister: Maryam Monsef's Meteoric Rise to Power and her Spectacular Fall From Grace

Maryam Monsef is the ultimate immigrant success story. She could not speak English when she arrived in Canada at age eleven. Two decades later she became Canada's first Muslim Cabinet Minister.

Maryam Monsef's story begins with her mother, a young Afghan widow who fled Afghanistan for Canada with her three young daughters in 1995. That widow spoke English but her three daughters did not. They brought something far more valuable to Canada: the unshakeable belief they could accomplish anything they wanted, so long as they worked hard.

It's no accident her belief in herself led Maryam Monsef to a Cabinet post. She worked hard to learn English and graduated from Trent University, an impossible accomplishment in her native Afghanistan.

Maryam Monsef became the unwitting scapegoat for Trudeau's broken promise on electoral reform, a promise he knew he would break by May 2016. Her birthplace controversy, her attempts to discredit and insult her electoral reform committee, combined with the Prime Minister's betrayal of her trust, sounded the death knell of her political career.

This, then, is the story of one young woman's meteoric rise to political power. It is also the story of that young woman's undoing at the hands of a narcissistic and self-serving celebrity feminist, Justin Trudeau.

https://ChristopherDiArmani.net/Maryam-Monsef-Book

Appendix - Daily Writing Routine Sample

I use a slightly different routine for each day of the week, based on tasks I know I must complete on specific days. The general shape of my daily routine, however, remains the same, with those specifics slotted in where and when needed.

1. Write for three hours.

I break this down into three separate Pomodoro sessions of two Pomodoros each. This is a psychological cheat I use to chunk down into the smallest component parts, each step of my day. Writing for two 25-minute sessions is easy. Writing for six 25-minute sessions seems more difficult, hence why I break it down into three separate sessions.

2. Read for 30 minutes - Writing Craft

I allow myself to read anything, so long as it is craft related. If it's a series of blog posts, great. If it's three chapters in a writing craft book, fantastic.

3. Read for 30 minutes - Genre-Specific

I write both fiction and non-fiction, but my genre-specific reading is always fiction. That's my personal choice. Yours may differ. As a result of my non-fiction writing research, I read a ton of non-fiction books, yet I don't count it here. Your routine and rationale for the choices made within it are your own, so don't lock yourself in to my decisions. See what works for you.

4. Personal Development for 1 hour.

Typically, this is where I listen to an audio book on a subject of interest. So long as it applies to making me a better person in some way, it counts. This includes listening to the Bible or Biblical commentators, too, since the Bible is the father of all self-help books, right?

This is the core of my work day.

It is also the bare minimum each day, not a maximum. Writing is my "day job" as well, so your daily routine probably looks very different. You may only write for 30 minutes each day because commuting and work take up the bulk of your time. No problem. The important thing is to ensure you include reading and writing somewhere in your daily routine.

Endnotes

1	Maslow, Abraham. "A Theory of Human Motivation." Psychological Review, 50, 370-396, 1943, http://psychclassics.yorku.ca/Maslow/motivation.htm. Accessed: Jan. 16, 2018.

2	Source: Text material adapted from D. Martin and K. Joomis, Building Teachers: A Constructivist Approach to Introducing Education, (Belmont, CA: Wadsworth, 2007), pp. 72-75.

3	Robbins, Tony. "6 Basic Needs That Make Us Tick." Entrepreneur Media, Inc, Undated, https://www.entrepreneur.com/article/240441. Accessed: Jan. 16, 2018.

4	Robbins, Tony. "Why we do what we do." Robbins Research International, Inc., Sept. 16, 2016, https://www.tonyrobbins.com/podcasts/why-we-do-what-we-do/. Accessed: Jan. 16, 2018.

5	Duhigg, Charles. "The Power of Habit: Why We Do What We Do in Life and Business." Random House, 2012. Kindle Edition

6	Tracy, Brian. "No Excuses! The Power of Self-Discipline." Vanguard Press, 2011. Kindle Edition

7	Ward, Marguerite. "Richard Branson says this daily habit doubles his productivity." CNBC.com, Nov. 10, 2016, https://www.cnbc.com/2016/11/10/richard-branson-says-this-daily-habit-doubles-his-productivity.html. Accessed: Jan. 06, 2018.

8	Smith, Dave. "7 Benefits of Morning Exercise, Plus 5 Tricks To Actually Love It." MakeYourBodyWork.com, Undated, https://makeyourbodywork.com/benefits-of-morning-exercise/. Accessed: Jan. 09, 2018.

9	Fox, Kenneth R.. "The influence of physical activity on mental well-being." Journal of Public Health Nutrition, Volume 2, Issue 3a, March 1999, pp. 411-418, https://doi.org/10.1017/S1368980099000567. Accessed: Jan. 09, 2018.

10	ASU News. "Early morning exercise is best for reducing blood pressure and improving sleep." Appalacian State University News, June 13, 2011, http://www.news.appstate.edu/2011/06/13/early-morning-exercise/. Accessed: Jan. 09, 2018.

11	Murray, Jacqui. "Word Count by Genre." Jacqui Murray's WordDreams Blog, December 8, 2010, https://worddreams.wordpress.com/2010/12/08/word-count-by-genre/. Accessed: Jan. 03, 2018.

12	Sambuchino, Chuck. "Word Count for Novels and Children's Books: The Definitive Post." WritersDigest.com, October 24, 2012, http://www.writersdigest.com/editor-blogs/guide-to-literary-agents/word-count-for-novels-and-childrens-books-the-definitive-post. Accessed: Jan. 03, 2018.

13	Blue. "Great Novels and Word Count." Indefeasible.WordPress.com, May 3, 2008, https://indefeasible.wordpress.com/2008/05/03/great-novels-and-word-count/. Accessed: Jan. 16, 2018.

14	Matthews, Dr. Gail. "Study demonstrates that writing goals enhances goal achievement." Dominican University of California, Jan. 5, 2017, https://www.dominican.edu/dominicannews/study-demonstrates-that-writing-goals-enhances-goal-achievement. Accessed: Jan. 18, 2018.

www.ingramcontent.com/pod-product-compliance
Lightning Source LLC
Chambersburg PA
CBHW070858050426
42453CB00012B/2253